FLOWERS
REDISCOVERED

FLOWERS REDISCOVERED

NEW IDEAS FOR USING AND ENJOYING FLOWERS

BY

MÄDDERLAKE

TOM PRITCHARD
BILLY JARECKI AND
ALAN BOEHMER

STEWART, TABORI & CHANG, PUBLISHERS
NEW YORK

PAGE 1:
The inspiration for Mädderlake's name.

PAGE 2:
The bounty of a late-summer garden: green-apple branches, wild sweet peas with pea pods, eustoma, phlox, cosmos, coreopsis, garden roses. lythrum, kerria, hydrangea, and honeysuckle.

PAGE 5:
Drenched sunflowers.

PAGE 8:
Flowers from late spring: checker-board lilies, peppermint-stick tulips, wild columbine, blood-red peony tulip, blue ajuga, mixed daffodils, and a leggy blue hyacinth.

FOR MARYJANE AND FOR LEO
AND ESPECIALLY FOR GINGER

PREFACE

Flowers. Creatures of pure and extraordinary beauty, composed of varieties so vast as to be virtually unknowable to the ordinary mortal.

Endless numbers of shapes, colors and combinations of colors, sizes, and fragrances make up this boundless kingdom, so it seems impossible that, for most of us, the words "fresh flowers" bring to mind so few images: an iris or two, some blue statice, white daisies, and a sprig of babies'-breath, all tightly rolled into a cone of florist's paper; galvanized buckets filled with sprays of gladiolas, red and white carnations, rubrum lilies, and brightly toned African daisies; a single rose paired with a fern leaf.

Flowers Rediscovered takes a closer look at a much wider world of flowers. We examine what cut flowers really are, and, to our mind, what they are not; where they can come from, how we can use them, even what they might come to mean in our lives. But first who are we, and where did we come from?

Mädderlake began quite by accident in 1975. An offbeat and neglected little plant store in Greenwich Village, recently transformed by its owner with an incongruous coat of shiny aluminum paint, stood in dire need of rescue. Alan and Billy had worked in that store and had grand ideas about what it could become; the architect in me sensed the possibility of creating something special here.

We sold Christmas trees from the sidewalk to raise a little cash to get started, then renovated the store ourselves, creating two water gardens surrounded by gently curved natural wood walls dappled by sunlight all day long. We combed the surrounding countryside for interesting and unusual plants and flowers, a routine we still observe in order to keep our store constantly supplied with intriguing things. Our forays often took us several hundred miles from New York, to dozens of small mom-and-pop greenhouses located on side roads, each having a treasure or two to yield: wooden grape crates filled with field-dug English daisies; fragrant yellow, white, and even pink jasmines; elegant calla lily plants over five feet tall; strange and wondrous kinds of hanging ceropegia and rhipsalis.

For containers, we scoured the backyards of these places, turning up old crates, boxes of all sorts, and clay pots, discarded long ago, now encrusted with mosses, lichens, and salts. We discovered how to marry a particular plant to a particular container so that each offering was unique. We learned, for instance, that in the middle of New York City, a dandelion planted in a tiny strawberry crate can be seen as a rare flower; that a tuft of nutgrass, unremarkable under ordinary conditions, when singled out and given an appropriate pot, has its own special beauty.

The New York Times described the store as a tropical paradise espousing new ideas and fresh ways of looking at and using plants and flowers. And when the limousines from uptown began pulling up to our door and our deliveries for the most part were headed for the Upper East Side, we realized that it was time to move and grow. Rather than adapting ourselves to the elegance of our new surroundings—68th and Madison—we brought our down-to-earth style with us. Mädderlake became a little oasis on Madison, a casual, mossy-bricked retreat from the world of haute couture and expensive jewelry, bevelled mirrors and polished brass.

Because we came to the world of flowers by chance rather than by design, we arrived with a fairly clean slate: neither had we been schooled in the art of floral design, nor had we been apprenticed to a particular tradition. Rather than seeing flowers as needing to be wired, woven, tied, or worked into unnatural configurations, we learned to recognize what was special about each kind of flower and how to work with that quality. While this may not appear at first to be a revolutionary premise, even a casual glance at what is being produced commercially demonstrates that this simple and natural approach does run directly against the prevailing floral winds. In fact, most of us know flower arrangements only from the often stiff and formal work we see in flower shops, work which would seem to need to be learned somewhere.

This book suggests a different approach. Rather than offering a style to emulate, or a step-by-step method to follow, it suggests a simple approach, an easygoing attitude, to the whole process. Armed with an understanding of a few basic notions underlying each part of the process of working with flowers, the rest becomes a simple matter of choice and evaluation.

Change seems to be in the air for the flower industry. As our ideas and attitudes regarding health and fitness, food, drink, and social interaction are changing and becoming more generous, more thoughtful, and more expansive, our notions of flowers seem to be following suit.

Most of us see the world around us as learned ideas and images which, for the most part, we tend to accept with little question. This is how it must be, of course, for it would be exhausting and thoroughly confusing to be constantly challenging and reinventing everything around us. However, when we find that our perception of any part of our world is severely limited, questionable at best, it would seem time to take a fresh new look. Perhaps for flowers, now is such a time.

Tom Pritchard

CONTENTS

CHAPTER ONE : SIGNIFICANCE

We could easily survive without flowers.

In the natural world, of course, their role is essential. A flower's appearance as casual ornament is a simple deception, as we well know, for it is the purpose of the flower to ensure the continuation of its species.

Flowers provide no such service for us. They do not give us nourishment or shelter. We don't actually *need* them to live our lives. Yet they have developed a great deal of significance for us, and we do seem to have a need for them—on a fairly regular basis for some of us, and at special moments, at least, for most. Perhaps the very fact that flowers are not directly necessary to our survival allows us to imbue them with abstract meanings.

Struck by the incredible beauty and vitality of flowers, we have given them roles that transcend mere decoration. Throughout antiquity and well into this century, flowers have held important and sometimes complex meanings in various societies. Even today, while few of the specific meanings survive, a handful of enduring associations persists.

Since the days of ancient Greece and Rome, flowers have performed an important symbolic function in culture and literature. Narcissus and Hyacinthus were both, according to classical mythology, half-divine, half-human creatures who were transformed into flowers when they died. Both the narcissus and the hyacinth are flowers of spring, and their myths underscore a key association between the rebirth of the earth in the spring and the flowers that herald it. Daffodils, jonquils, crocuses, snowdrops, and glory-of-the-snow as well all seem to embody the notion of spring renewal. It is not surprising that with the bleakness of winter at its harshest, the sight of a single flower can conjure up the whole image of spring in the mind's eye.

Other flowers are also traditionally associated with the greening of the earth and the dissolution of winter's mantle: the tiny pink flowers of the redbud, often the only spot of early color in the damp, gray woods; early azaleas, which flower long before their leaves emerge; the sunny little winter aconite; patches of pale blue scilla siberica; and simple white flowers of the bloodroot. The theme of rebirth

Crocus in the garden—one of the first signs of spring. Like many other spring flowers—hyacinths, lilies, daffodils, narcissus—crocuses have come to suggest both the physical and the spiritual promise of life triumphant over death.

Narcissus breaks through winter's blanket of cold and gloom. When paper-whites are forced to bloom indoors in midwinter, their delicate purity and sweet-sharp scent remind us of spring as few things can.

culminates, for some, in the appearance of the tall, graceful white lilies at Easter, symbols not only of purity and innocence but of the triumph of life over death—a spiritual rebirth parallel to that of the earth itself. In addition, the venerable rite of dancing and exchanging gifts of flowers on May Day and the custom of giving lilies-of-the-valley at a christening are occasions when flowers betoken life, birth, fertility, and renewal.

During the Middle Ages and the Renaissance, a so-called language of flowers began to figure in courtly behavior. The plays of Shakespeare are filled with references to flowers. Ophelia, gone mad from unrequited love for Hamlet, speaks in riddles:

> There's rosemary, that's for remembrance. Pray you, love, remember. And
> there is pansies, that's for thoughts....There's fennel for you, and colum-
> bines. There's rue for you, and here's some for me.

The assignment of precise meanings to certain flowers reached a peak in Victorian England. A little book published in 1913, *The Language of Flowers*, lists more than 700 blooms with their respective significances. We find, for example, that the garden anemone stands for forsakenness; the evening primrose, inconstancy; the olive, peace; lavender, distrust; and the veronica, fidelity. Oddly enough, the mouse-eared scorpion grass signifies "forget me not," while the forget-me-not itself stands for true love. A yellow rose still carries connotations of jealousy to many people, although few such rigid correspondences have survived.

"O, my luve is like a red, red rose..." Burns knew it, and so do we: the single red rose remains an enduring token of true love. In early Christian iconography, the rose was often a symbol of Christ's love, but the earthly and the divine have conveniently combined over the centuries. The ancients believed that the red rose was stained by Venus's blood when her finger was wounded by one of its thorns. In pagan Rome, roses were synonymous with orgies, indulgence, and lust. According to legend, Cleopatra had her mattresses stuffed with fresh roses every night. Horace mentions, in describing a typical palace banquet scene, that it was Roman custom to adorn the statues of the gods with crowns of roses while naked dancers of both sexes, festooned with long garlands of garden roses, danced amid the guests. Nero allegedly caused such enormous quantities of rose petals to be rained down on the heads of his dinner guests that overindulgent diners were occasionally suffocated.

Today, a rose—especially, it seems, a red one—speaks, somewhat more amiably, for the heart at the first rendezvous, at a wedding, on an anniversary, on the spur of the moment, and especially on the day of declared love, St. Valentine's.

While the single rose speaks of love, a rambling rose conjures up not an emotion but a place—England—and its country gardens overrun with ancient, twisted multiflora roses. This association has a long history, which perhaps reached its height during the fifteenth century, when the flower appeared in the heraldic emblems of the kingdom's reigning families and gave its name to their bitter conflict, the Wars of the Roses. Other flowers also have regional associations. For example, who can think of rows and rows of tulips without visions of Holland immediately coming to mind? Similarly, magnolias conjure up images of the Deep South; cherry blossoms, both Japan and Washington, D.C.; a lei of orchids, indisputably, Hawaii.

In one or two rare cases, a flower has developed a strong and lasting association with an individual personality. Dumas's *La Dame aux Camélias* is perhaps the most illustrious of all; her fragile beauty is emblematically identified with the equally delicate camellia flower she wore without fail. Billie Holiday also came to be symbolized by a flower, like her, easily bruised and short-lived—the pure and fragrant gardenia bloom. And of course there's that *femme fatale* of the Pacific, the seductive Tokyo Rose—so named, it is said, because her voice gave off attar of roses, while her message stung like a thorn.

"Flores...Flores para los muertos...." With these chilling lines George, in Edward Albee's *Who's Afraid of Virginia Woolf*, sets the stage for announcing to his wife, Martha, the "death" of their "son." With an armload of snapdragons, apparently a gift for Martha, George initiates the final encounter of the evening. Unaware of

PAGES 16–17:
A moment of childhood loss: the passage in the classic story *Toby Tyler* where his beloved monkey, Mr. Stubbs, dies. Toby feels compelled to leave wildflowers on the newly dug grave.

George's deadly intentions, Martha accepts his offering of flowers as a request for a truce in the night's ghastly proceedings. George skillfully nurtures this perception until he has Martha at her most vulnerable. Then, with a particularly evil game called "snap goes the dragon," in which George hurls the flowers one by one at Martha as he brings her the dread news, the hapless young innocent is mercilessly "killed" and the true meaning of the flowers as "flowers for the dead" is finally realized.

Albee's masterful scene underscores the fact that flowers are as inextricably interwoven with our notions of death as they are with our expressions of love; the last symbolic connection between the living and the dead is often made with flowers. Perhaps our need to express the unity of life and death causes us to surround the event of a death with visual associations of life. While the loveliness of the life just passed should be represented by the flowers, these are, in far too many cases, done by rote and as a result look ponderous and overdone. Even so, poignant gestures do occur—none more touching, perhaps, than the laying of a single flower onto a casket moments before it is lowered into the ground, or the scattering of flowers over the waves following a burial at sea.

In some mystical, spiritual way, we imbue flowers with the power to speak for us beyond the grave. We often carry flowers to graveside and leave them behind, a reminder of the visit, a tangible connection between the living and the dead. Other forms of homage to the dead are expressed through flowers as well. The poppy, or typically a rather crudely fashioned paper likeness, worn in the lapel each Veterans' Day, is an expression of national and personal remembrance. A symbolic reminder of the poppies that blanketed the World War I battlefields of Flanders, these fragile paper flowers attest that the gallant soldiers now gone are remembered by those who survive.

On a somewhat grander scale, public homage is signified by placing a wreath of flowers at the tomb of an unknown soldier, an event that always seems to play a well-publicized role in state visits. Thus do heads of state acknowledge one another's right to mourn the war dead, even if they have not acknowledged the right to the war.

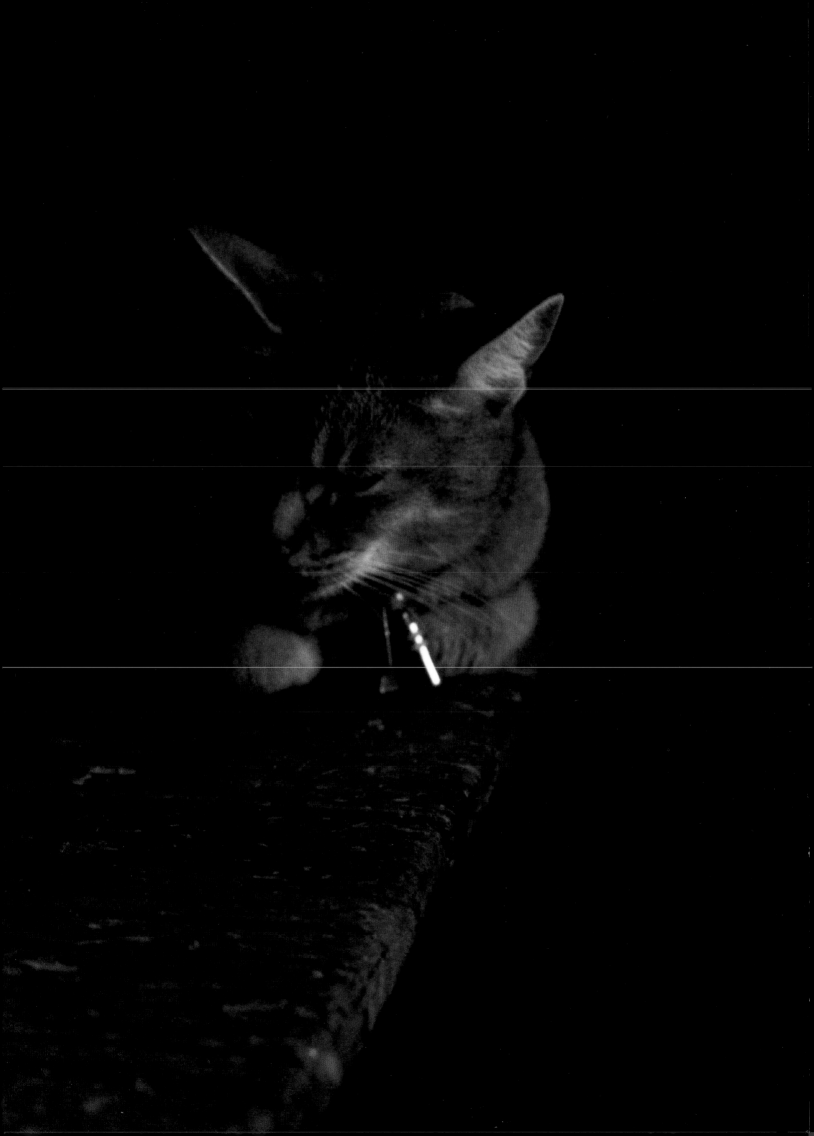

LEFT:
Left amid the pine needles and fallen leaves of a country graveyard are rambling roses, anemones, and white nerines.

BELOW:
A few roses at graveside—an emblematic connection between the living and the dead.

BOTTOM:
Anemones, pumpkin lilies, scabious, and ranunculus adorn a quiet grave.

DIED
April 14, 1874,
Aged years;
9 mo 23 days.
orgotten.
away.

In his charming but compelling fable, *The Story of Ferdinand*, published in 1936, Munro Leaf wrote of a young bull who desired only to sit in the shade of his favorite tree and smell the soft, sweet scents of the meadow flowers. Unlike the other young bulls, all blindly eager to perform for the crowds, Ferdinand's inclination was against conflict. When the time finally came for him to enter the ring and face the matador, Ferdinand walked out to the center and simply sat down, content to smell the perfume from the flowers that all the ladies in the stands wore in their hair. Although the tale is lighthearted in tone, Leaf has provided us with an enduring metaphoric connection between flowers and peace.

The link between flowers and peace gained new prominence in the 1960s. A generation of young people in rebellion against the militaristic policies of their country came to be known as "flower children"; the strength of their movement, "flower power." Images abounded of barefoot and disheveled youths with simple garlands of field flowers about their necks and in their hair, of impromptu outdoor weddings and love-ins with flowers scattered all about. Perhaps the most evocative image was that of a small daisy being placed into the barrel of a fiercely bayoneted gun.

LEFT:
Snowdrops—as white as the snow they presage an end to.

PAGES 22–23:
Flowers can heighten an event. White roses and gerbera daisies make this children's birthday party playful and festive.

LEFT:
A gift of flowers can convey so many different messages. Sometimes, words fail us, but perhaps the eloquent entreaty of this bouquet—callas, amaryllis, roses, poppies, quince, and French lilac— will make the right apology, and win forgiveness.

Finally, flowers are the universal expression of tribute. Throughout history, flowers have been showered on heroes and strewn at the feet of the victorious. Far-flung images come to mind: the giant horseshoe-shaped wreath presented to the winning horse at the Kentucky Derby; the armloads of roses carried by Miss America, Miss Universe, and myriad other beauty queens. Laurel wreaths have crowned Olympic athletes, and bouquets and scattered flowers are rained down on triumphant divas at La Scala and other opera houses the world over. These exuberant offerings are universal in meaning, if not always in beauty, once more conveying a significance far beyond their mere form.

ABOVE:
Sterling silver and champagne roses, white lilac, crispa, and pink striated nerines compose this Biedermeier-inspired bit of nostalgia.

Along with wild applause and shouts of "Bravo!," the flowers thrown at the feet of an opera star and the bouquets from fans are age-old expressions of approval, love, and gratitude. Dancers, matadors, and actors also receive the accolade of flowers—and what could be a more fitting honor, since flowers are nature's own extravagant praise of herself?

CHAPTER TWO : CHANGE

It is a flower's nature to change.

Its life is shorter than a year, shorter even than a season. A flower appears, more briefly and more poignantly than almost anything else in nature, and then vanishes.

Sometimes this brief life lasts a week or two, sometimes only a few days. Some flowers, such as garden flax or day lilies, bloom in the warmth of the early morning sun and fade completely by nightfall. The bloom of the hibiscus and of its northern cousin, the mallow flower, opens for just a single day and often falls to the floor in a crumpled heap by the next morning. One variety of hibiscus is referred to as "flower-of-an-hour" or "goodnight-at-noon" because its flowers completely finish blooming by midday. The buds of the neomarica, more commonly known as "walking iris," swell for days in preparation for a few hours of glorious orchidlike perfection before twisting and turning into a faded corkscrew of debris.

The life of the night-blooming cereus is even briefer, and many a nocturnal sortie has been conducted to witness its elusive bloom. The gigantic bud, itself a totally

Flowers are inherently brief. As a rose blooms and fades, it changes dramatically, opening to a full, ravaged peak. It is equally beautiful at all stages, from bud to potpourri—which, after all, is simply another kind of flower arrangement.

The fragile Christmas rose blooms only briefly in the dark days of winter.

improbable emergence from the flat, succulent tails of the plant, swells for days, sometimes weeks. Then one night, in complete darkness, the bud explodes in a spectacular display. A dazzling flower bursts open to almost three times its original size and survives for an hour or two, perhaps three, only to fall, spent and bedraggled, by the light of early morning. This dramatic sequence reveals a mysterious power and beauty that only flowers born of brevity possess. We are forced by the very nature of such flowers to consider them more closely: their impermanence adds a dimension that we simply do not find in flowers that endure.

❦

We have been conditioned to want our money's worth from everything we buy, but especially, it seems, from flowers; "longer lasting" has come to be regarded as "better." Hence the flower industry's reliance on the war horses of the trade: chrysanthemums, carnations, gladiolas, babies'-breath, statice, anthuriums, gingers, and the like. Not only do most of these flowers remain in bloom for a relatively long time, they also rarely exhibit any perceptible change; indeed, many varieties of these flowers have been hybridized specifically to remain unchanging. There is no surprise in store, nothing for the flower to *become*.

And therein lies the rub. There is nothing to be gained from watching these flowers over time. While so many other flowers only gradually reveal themselves, these flowers, for the most part, just stay put. Many of them actually begin to rot internally long before they actually fade.

This is not to say that carnations, chrysanthemums, and the others are never beautiful; of course they can be. But depending on these few flowers has made the flower industry all too predictable and limiting for producer and consumer alike. And the industry is now thoroughly set in its ways and likely to remain so, unless pressure is brought to bear on it from outside its ranks.

The apotheosis, or possibly the *reductio ad absurdum*, of the long-life principle is silk flowers. These replicas never live, never need attention (except, perhaps, dusting), and consequently, however clever the mimicry, have absolutely nothing to do with

what makes a flower a flower. No matter how beautiful these objects may be, there is no breath, no animating spirit, no change.

❦

A carnation stays white and stays white until, one day, it turns brown; an anthurium flower remains unchanged until it cracks and dries up. But the more interesting flowers have dramatic life cycles, with beginnings, middles, and ends. Watching a flower realize its full metamorphosis is a real pleasure. A trumpet lily's tightly held bloom exposes its insides one day, revealing a wine-soaked throat and elegant anthers laden with deep yellow pollen. An anemone's flower unfurls in daylight and warmth and closes again with the cool of evening; an amaryllis's flower swells from a small bud to an enormous, deep-throated blossom; a belladonna lily emerges from a tight, papery sheath and shoots its cluster of pink flowers into the light.

Perhaps no flower changes more dramatically than the poppy. Irving Penn, in his book *Flowers*, explores the many subtle nuances of the life cycle of poppies and of peonies, lilies, roses, and a few other flowers. In a rhapsodic sequence of photographs, Penn captures the different kinds of beauty that a poppy exhibits at different points in its life—from its inception as a sealed sheath, to a small green bud, to the unmistakable finality of its fallen petals, scattered pollen, and sentrylike remains.

The rose is another flower that is ravishing at all stages of its life. From bud to first blush to full-blown to over-blown to faded petals to potpourri, a rose offers an ecstatic visual performance. Perhaps it is because the rose is such an attractive argument for mortality that its cycle has often been used metaphorically to describe human life.

But there are also many striking flowers whose lives are almost too short to be chronicled. These flowers of legend and literature seem to hold a permanent and very special place in our hearts, yet they are almost impossible to find outside of

country gardens and fields. Violets, pansies, and English daisies, jack-in-the-pulpit, lily-of-the-valley, wild sweet peas, and the very fragile Christmas rose—these flowers are exquisite but very brief presences. The forget-me-not, another exceedingly fleeting flower, explicitly reminds us that a beautiful moment does not have to cease simply because it has passed; its sweetness, like youth and first love, survives in the memory.

Our realization that this vast, virtually untapped world of flowers can be enjoyed daily depends on some acknowledgment of these notions of temporal change. We must accept the fact that flowers do not have to last in order to have value for us. We must recognize that often their beauty inheres in their brevity and in their ability to grow, develop, and change.

Roses—with their beautiful excess
and noble decline, they provide an
ideal metaphor for our own lives.

CHAPTER THREE : CHARACTER

An arrangement of flowers is successful if its various elements work together.

Each individual flower, however strong its character, should be considered first in terms of its contribution to the whole, for when any one flower clearly dominates, the harmony of the arrangement is upset. The way to achieve a proper balance of flowers is to understand the impact each will have on the entire composition.

The attributes of an individual flower can easily be recognized and evaluated, and its most fitting use thereby determined. Generally speaking, flowers that are very assertive in one way or another tend to resist combination, while those of a more subtle disposition mix more readily. A flower typically has one or two characteristics that are clearly dominant and therefore dictate how it can best be used.

Color, size, and shape head the list of these determining factors. The electric blue of a delphinium, for instance, is a real force to be reckoned with. This flower is also large and distinctively shaped, making it a doubly strong presence; a deft hand is required to combine it successfully with others. On the other hand, a soft pink larkspur, though also distinctive in size and shape, lends itself more easily to combination, due to its more muted colors and smaller individual flowers. An amaryllis flower is, first and foremost, massive. Its color and shape are overshadowed by its size, which completely governs its usability. As a result, except in overscaled arrangements, amaryllis is hard to combine with other flowers.

A flower's shape also contributes directly to its purpose in an arrangement. Since a variety of forms are needed to produce an interesting combination, it is important to understand which flowers are likely to contribute the shapes necessary to round out a mixed arrangement.

Many flowers have relatively straight stems. These form the backbone of an arrangement, for they provide the structure against which more interestingly shaped flowers may be placed. Roses, snapdragons, stock, viburnum, larkspur, lilies, daffodils, tuberoses, nerines, and hybrid lilacs, to name but a few, most often have straight stems. The stems of tulips, on the other hand, are almost always bent and curved

The vine lily known as the gloriosa has a graceful, somewhat streamlined shape and vivid coloring. It adapts well to other flowers and lends racy elegance to almost any arrangement.

and, along with ranunculus, poppies, freesia, dendrobium orchids, Euphorbia fulgens, Rothschild lilies, and hyacinths, help to fill out an arrangement, keeping it from becoming too upright or too rigid, lending it fullness, softness, lyricism, and grace.

Perhaps the opposite characteristics are typical of the dense clusters of the mimosa's flowers and leaves. Like wild babies'-breath, feverfew, and some kinds of heather, the mimosa has a way of overwhelming other flowers, quickly filling up the interior of an arrangement and leaving little room for the variety of flowers needed for a full mix. While wonderful in their own right, the visual density of these flowers poses a problem when they are combined with others.

Some flowers, such as gladiolas, liatris, desert candles, and some irises, are spiky and, except in extremely large arrangements, resist combination with softer, more rounded flowers. They seem to shoot out of the arrangement, disrupting rather than supporting its unity. These flowers are often more easily used on their own. Flowering quince, dogwood, magnolia, and other ornamental shrubs and trees contribute shapely branches, which not only secure an arrangement and give it a foundation but also provide contrasting angular shapes against which other flowers can be positioned.

Temporal change (see Chapter 2) should be anticipated as well. One should allow room for those flowers that are going to develop substantially over time. Certain flowers, such as gerbera daisies, calla lilies, anthuriums, carnations, zinnias, and most orchids remain virtually unchanged from the day they are picked until they finally die. But others change radically from start to finish, such as: poppies; garden, eucharist, and belladonna lilies; velouta and other amaryllislike flowers; and various nerines. From bud to flower, a rose develops to more than three times its original size, and space must be provided for it to do so. The stems of tulips, hyacinths, and other flowers cut from spring bulbs will actually elongate, moving, twisting, and growing over the course of a few days, some almost doubling their initial length.

Tropical flowers, such as various protea, gingers, birds-of-paradise, and anthuriums are sometimes highly specific, relentless flowers—assertive, self-conscious, even garish.

A burst of short-lived clusters of soft yellow flowers amid the dense yet fragile-looking bed of gray-green foliage—such are the contradictory charms of the mimosa flower.

LEFT:
The spiky stalks of the delphinium are softened by their clusters of puffy blue flowers. The delphinium is assertive without being aggressive—like words pronounced very clearly in a soft tone of voice.

BELOW:
Queen Anne's lace is fragile and shapely. Its distinctive umbrella crown and long, curved stem give it a regal appearance. A common meadow bloom, Queen Anne's lace has also been selectively bred for larger size. The flowers shown here are of the hybrid garden variety.

PAGES 46–47:
Sandersonii, like mimosa, is a densely foliated, distinctive flower that tends to look best on its own. To work with other flowers, its foliage needs to be thinned out.

While extremely long-lived, these jungle flowers tend not to mix well with those from a temperate climate and are most often combined with giant philodendron leaves, which, in nature, grow in their midst. Or one sees them placed in strange, often unappealing configurations with bamboo poles, branches of corkscrew willow, Spanish moss, fan-palm leaves, and other exotic paraphernalia.

Other tropical flowers, however, have more in common with their northern neighbors and so can add delight and surprise to more traditional mixes of flowers. Bougainvillaea, plumbago, mandevilla, flowering begonias, jasmine, and mimosa all come from the warmer zones, as does the extremely beautiful and versatile Rothschild lily. Although this flower is by no means retiring—it sports a vivid red color outlined in bright yellow, and has a striking shape—it mixes splendidly with other flowers. Its vining nature produces many different stem shapes, allowing it to be placed virtually anywhere in an arrangement, while the flower itself seems curiously independent, often appearing to be flying through space. It is this wonderful sense of movement and drama that makes the tropical Rothschild lily so intriguing and flexible to work with.

RIGHT:
Even a calla lily can soften up in
the right context. Here, the flowers
seem almost whimsical.

In addition to these observable characteristics, the moods and images that some flowers can evoke also become part of their contribution to an arrangement. Bulbs produce flowers that are reminiscent of spring: light and delicate jonquils, daffodils, and miniature narcissus, glory-of-the-sun, tiny grape hyacinths, and, of course, tulips of all sorts. An "English garden" mood is evoked by many flowers picked from the herbaceous borders of our summer gardens: foxglove and delphinium, larkspur, bee balm, trumpet lilies, and tall, elegant cleome flowers. Branches and shade-loving wildflowers such as trillium, jack-in-the-pulpit, false Solomon's-seal, lady's-slipper, Canada lilies, and bloodroot are "woodsy" in feeling; whereas black-eyed Susan, clover, Shirley poppies, wild snapdragons, field daisies, and Queen Anne's lace suggest sunny summer meadows.

But perhaps nothing conjures up images of times and places long gone by quite like the fragrance that certain flowers give off. The heady aroma of dark purple lilacs hanging heavy on a still night, the sweet smell of jasmine carried inland by a sea breeze, the soft, deep aroma of a gardenia laden with ripening flowers, the essence of lily-of-the-valley redolent of the woods, the earthy nectar of garden roses—all are endowed with a subliminal power to lift our spirits and refresh our memories.

The classically elegant calla lily is extremely linear and assertive, and can hold its own in any setting. It reached its height of popularity in the 1930s, when it appeared in countless Hollywood movies as an emblem of drop-dead glamour.

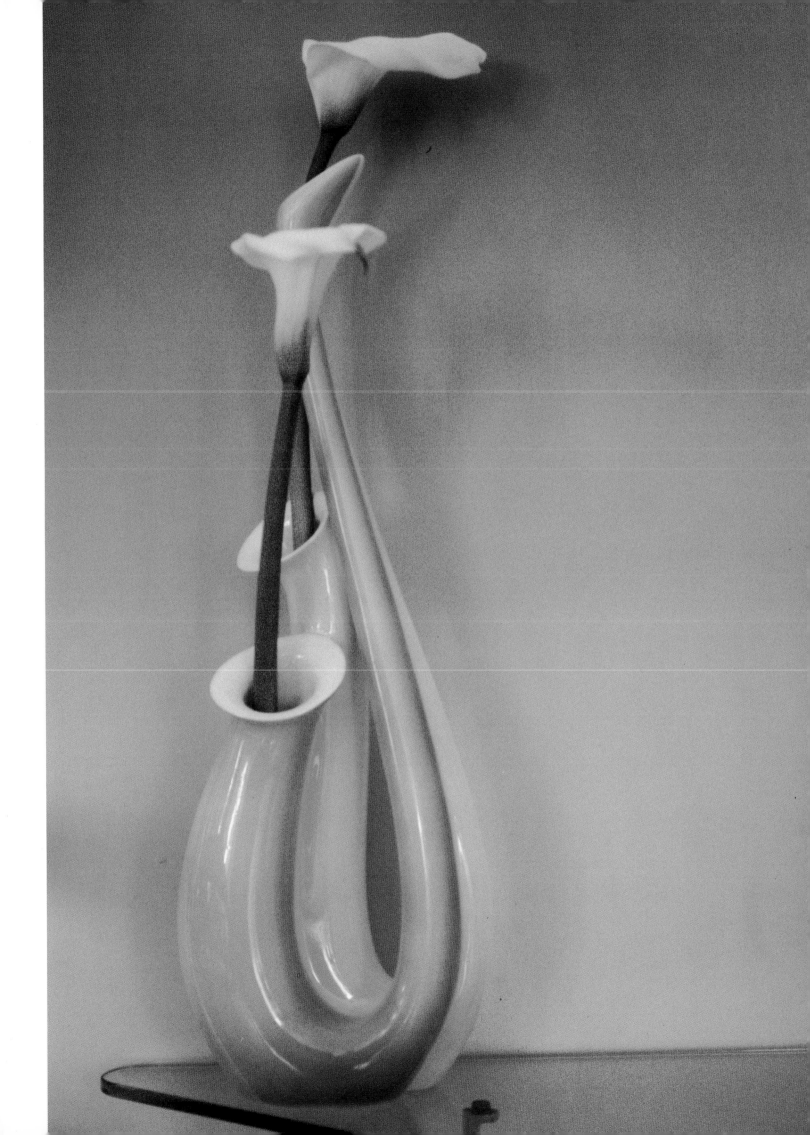

LEFT:
Vibrant color and aggressive shape—the gladiolus has both. Because it's so assertive, it often looks best when not combined with other flowers, and in a vase that can stand up to it.

RIGHT:
The bizarre effusion of these enormous drooping ginger fingers easily dominates a room.

PAGES 56–57:
The stems of tulips (and of many other flowers from spring bulbs) will actually elongate over time. Hence their arching, drooping silhouettes, their languorous quality of movement.

PAGES 58–59:
Flowers with very different growth habits can work together. The curved, stretching stems of the tulips and the varying stem shapes of the Rothschild lilies help round out the underside of this mixed arrangement.

ABOVE:
A bowl of snowdrops in early springtime—simplicity itself.

LEFT:
Tall, elegant tulips are grown in the south of France.

CHAPTER FOUR : SOURCE AND RESOURCE

Florists are the most obvious source for flowers.

The best florists are those who are willing to increase the scope of what flowers are available, to expand the range of possibilities. After all, the tall bundles of electric blue delphiniums; the infinite colors of fringed, peony, and parrot tulips; the sterling silver, champagne, and shocking blue roses; California and Oriental poppies; and the elegant, long, leafless stems of pale lavender and white French lilac all come, for the most part, from the same wholesale sources as do the pom-pom mums, glads, and carnations that fill the average florist's cooler. It's mostly a matter of choice—and vision.

Unfortunately, many florists operate lackluster shops that are interested primarily in profits and, therefore, maintaining the status quo. In order to help sell an uninspired selection of flowers, they invent all sorts of clever paper and plastic gimmicks: coffee mugs, leprechauns, papier mâché hearts, and reusable tote bags are some of the notions that are served up to customers along with flowers. The idea that flowers are just one more commodity to be bought and sold does little to inspire those searching for the real delights that flowers have to offer.

In some cities and towns, however, more sophisticated flower shops have appeared, shops known as "boutique" or sometimes "carriage-trade" florists. Here the range of flowers is far greater, the quality is superior, and the florists are willing to go to almost any lengths to satisfy an often knowledgeable and always demanding clientele. Taking their cue from the great shops of London and Paris, these proprietors seek to exploit the natural inclinations of the flowers themselves and have begun to use flowers in more inventive and subtle ways. The results have been noteworthy, and the ideas that these florists espouse are slowly beginning to trickle into the mainstream.

Market forces in these cities have been stimulated by this turn of events. In New York, for example, the wholesale flower market, thanks to repeated demands from these florists, has developed a voracious appetite for the unusual; new varieties of plants and flowers, as well as bundles of cuttings from the woods and fields, appear with great regularity. Before the sun is up, there is often a scramble for

Using what is available can result in happy combinations, such as these flowers in a white squash, hollowed out and used as a vase. An odd little aloe flower, nasturtiums, and herbs—meadow rue, leafy sage, rosemary, and lemon thyme—have a timeless quality when arranged together. The faded Chinese lantern on the table is the fruit of a vine that grows wild and is also a garden cultivar.

the two or three bunches of something really special that happened to hit the market that morning. Reputations are made and maintained by the types of new and different flowers a shop can offer to its regular customers. In the five or six months of just one winter season, for example, the New York flower market saw the appearance of elegant lizzianthus flowers; a variety of tall and strange flower stems from succulent kalanchoe plants; the graceful, three-foot-tall tulips from the south of France; flowers from the buddleia bush; jack-in-the-pulpits; tiny calla lilies (first the deep yellow ones, then the pink ones that shade from a pale color to a rather sinister burgundy); boxes of forget-me-nots; and tiny hybrid Queen Anne's lace.

In addition to the standard wholesale distributors, sellers in station wagons ply their trade up and down the avenues, loaded with rare flowers grown in backyard gardens and small greenhouses and also cut from the wild. A simple principle is at work here: supply and demand. Once a demand is voiced, a supply will be found.

In the Mädderlake shop, the variety of flowers available in late fall is astonishing. Pictured here are orchids, lilies, roses, narcissus, bachelor's-buttons, purple callicarpa branches, liatris, Queen Anne's lace, tulips, nerines, wild daisies, and white skimmia flowers. Though difficult, it is not impossible for a flower shop to offer this kind of selection.

Berried branches cut from the
woods in autumn: bittersweet, crab
apples, wild rose hips.

Another source of a wide array of flowers is the increasingly popular farmers' markets, where garden flowers, weeds, and wildflowers are often sold side by side with freshly harvested vegetables and fruits. Those markets that don't sell flowers undoubtedly would if customers made a few inquiries, for rare are the truck farmers who don't have a splendid assortment of flowers for their own enjoyment and therefore the wherewithal to grow a few more for sale.

Produce stands as well have come to carry flowers more and more frequently in the past few years, although the quality certainly varies from stand to stand; understanding the needs of melons and tomatoes does not ensure that the owner of a fruit-and-vegetable stand knows how to treat flowers properly. Time may improve this situation, however, as more and more people come to regard flowers as an integral part of their lives. Varieties of flowers that just two or three years ago were available in only a handful of shops now sit alongside the more usual ones, ever increasing the range of what is accessible to greater numbers of people.

In more rural areas, the small roadside greenhouses offer the greatest hope. These family-run operations are a perfect source, for they have the built-in capability to produce small quantities of almost anything one might desire, without the over-whelming pressure that drives the commercial giants to grow only flowers with a proven track record. Furthermore, the owners of these greenhouses are generally eager to please, as well as genuinely interested in growing. Left on their own, these proprietors most often follow the national trends, filling their coolers with the ubiquitous gladiolas, anthuriums, and carnations, meanwhile surrounded by nurseries full of more interesting flowering plants and shrubs, all sorts of perennials in pots, hanging baskets laden with flowers, and greenhouses begging for exciting new crops to grow. All that they need are more articulate requests from their customers.

❧

Beyond these sources, a little imagination is called for. Resourcefulness becomes the operative word.

First, the flowers and branches of many pot-grown plants can be judiciously clipped

RIGHT:
Lythrum covers the fields of late summer with its lavender-red flowers.

BELOW:
Weeds gathered from the side of a dusty country road in summer: Queen Anne's lace, lythrum, and blue chicory. Learning to appreciate the conjunctions and profusions of color and shape that nature permits is an important step in understanding how to use flowers.

PAGES 68–69:
Among the picnic flowers bought at a roadside stand: blue globe thistle, snapdragons, yarrow, veronica, nasturtiums, strawberry flowers, ageratum, herbs and fruit, squash flowers, and painted daisies.

LEFT:
From the vegetable garden, a surprisingly graceful array: charentais melon, zucchini blossoms, grapes, purple eggplant flowers, and miniature red peppers.

BELOW:
A basketful of fall colors: crab apples, cleome, Chinese lanterns, coreopsis, Euphorbia fulgens, callicarpa, Rosa rugosa, and rose hips.

and used to great advantage, either alone or in arrangements. Azaleas, especially those which have gotten a bit leggy, add lushness and originality to a mix of other flowers. So do branches of calemondin orange (with flowers or fruit, or both); Jerusalem cherry, with its deep dark leaves and tomato-red fruit; fuchsia and branches of asparagus fern, especially those laden with green or ripe red berries; jasmines, allamanda, and snippings from bougainvillaea and plumbago; pieces of pomegranate with fruit and flowers; and cyclamen. Then, of course, there are camellias and geraniums, especially the pendant varieties of both, and stems of the richly colored rieger begonias. Most of these plants—only a few of the many possible candidates—can easily be purchased from a local greenhouse or florist.

Flower gardens hardly need be mentioned here. It is assumed that anyone with a garden recognizes its potential without having to be told. From the gardens of summer come tall blue scabiosa, hollyhocks, trumpet lilies, lupines, campanula, salpiglossis, montbretia, and thousands of others. All of these flowers, and many, many more, can make their way into the wholesale flower markets, often even in winter.

The one part of the garden that doesn't usually occur to people as a source of flowers, however, is the vegetable patch. Full of delightful, sometimes whimsical plants, this is definitely a place to raid from time to time for offbeat flowers and unusual bits and pieces. The blossom of an eggplant is as lovely as almost any other flower—a most delicate, pale shade of blue-lavender, with a vivid yellow center. A piece of the plant with tiny, dark eggplants hanging down works wonderfully in a flower arrangement, as do the young fruits and flowers of the tomato, melon,

LEFT:
Unexpected floral splendor from the vegetable garden: kale that has bolted in the heat of the summer.

ABOVE:
Many wonderful flowers grow in abundance in the herb garden—such as this blue salvia.

PAGES 74–75:
Purple and white lilacs. The abundant branches, the heady scent on the wind signal the start of summer.

LEFT:
Familiar but brilliant, dwarf zinnias from the garden look splendid in arrangements (above). The rangy coreopsis comes from a nursery—and cries out for pruning.

RIGHT:
Simplicity is one of the chief joys of summer flowers from field and garden. Here, the charm of alyssum, hollyhocks, rue, cosmos, marigold, and four-o'clock flowers.

PAGES 78–79:
One of the lushest and most romantic flowers, the peony is also one of the few flowers that cannot be grown outside of its natural season. Only once a year does its unrestrained extravagance enter our lives.

LEFT:
A mixed bouquet from a summer garden: black-eyed Susan, hollyhock—regular and miniature—blackberry lilies, cosmos, tomato flowers, and nasturtiums.

ABOVE:
A pink, blowsy diplademia flower being cut for use in an arrangement.

RIGHT:
A fairy-tale assemblage of flowers from the garden, fields, and woods: pendant geraniums, crab apple branches, zinnias, wild grapes, ageratum, woodland anemones, cosmos, and stephanotis.

ABOVE:
Garden roses.

and cucumber. Tomato flowers are an exquisite yellow, and when gathered profusely can make an impact; squash blossoms and melon flowers, while rather short-lived, are spectacular as well.

For those who live in the suburbs or the country, yards and fields often hold a vast array of possibilities that rarely come to mind when considering cut flowers for around the house. There are usually flowering trees, vines of all sorts, and shrubs that, if not really known for their flowers, do bloom at one time or another. Wisteria, trumpet vine, honeysuckle, and clematis are all rampant growers and big bloomers, and they even benefit from pruning. Rhododendrons and azaleas of all descriptions grace many lawns and hardly miss a few clipped-off branches. The list is almost endless: bridal wreath and other spireas, mock orange, quince, crab apple, weigela, mountain laurel (a protected plant in certain areas), abelia, and on and on. Pyracantha in the spring has dense clusters of soft, white flowers; in the fall, bright orange berries. A branch of young, green apples; stalks of kerria japonica with its soft, cadmium yellow flowers; and, of course, lilac, with its profusion of white and pale purple flowers and heady aroma—all are available just for the taking.

Even in the bleakest months, nature offers an abundance of materials. The ubiquitous sumac sports vivid carnival-colored leaves late into November (the smaller branches are usually more usable than the large ones), as does the intensely scarlet wing-barked euonymus and the thorny barberry, with its twisted branches and tiny

RIGHT:
A lotus flower dominates this casual arrangement of zinnias, cosmos, phlox, cleome, lilies, and crab apples.

Witch hazel blooms in the very coldest months, producing simple, densely clustered blossoms.

ABOVE:
Forsythia, deceived by the warmth of the autumn day, has begun to flower long before its time.

leaves. Most varieties of cotoneaster produce heavily berried branches; the rarer akebia offers clusters of bizarre, purple berries and small, shapely leaves. Myriad other woodland plants produce berries and seeds: hips from all sorts of roses, from the wild ramblers to the squat, fat beach roses; bittersweet; wild grapevines; privet; holly; and even Virginia creeper, with its dappled leaves and clusters of tiny berries. Certain kinds of witch hazel sport their flowers even in the very coldest months of the year. All of these, to name only a few, add real dimension to flowers of other kinds or are perfectly delightful by themselves.

In addition to the well-known white pine, balsam, and juniper, dozens of different kinds of evergreens grow across the country. Some boast tiny clusters of cones; others, soft, luxuriant boughs of greenery; still others, dramatic, angular branches and enormous, pointed cones jutting from them. The graceful, feathery Canadian hemlock, especially the more open-growing varieties (natural as opposed to shaped), is perfect to use as an interesting variation on the more conventional Christmas wreaths and garlands. Wreaths of powder-blue spruce, pachysandra, leucothoe, and the delicate blue Atlas cedar are only a few of the other possibilities, while the partridgeberry, with its diminutive leaves and few tiny red berries, makes perhaps the most delicate wreath of all.

Spring is the time for flowering branches. Very early on, the shadblow and the tiny redbud bloom, followed by forsythia, quince, magnolia, cornelian cherry, dogwood, apple, pear, and numerous others. Most of these branches can be forced earlier, in the winter. Once flowered branches have budded and gone through a long enough cold period (most branches can be safely cut by mid-January or so), they can be cut, put into water, and moved into a warm part of the house. Some city flower markets rely on forced branches as a staple for mid- to late-winter flowers, with white and pink quince and forsythia arriving around Thanksgiving, followed by magnolia in late January, and finally dogwood in the first weeks of March.

Early spring is also the time for bulbs (which can also be forced indoors during the winter months simply by providing water), and this great source of flowers that

Flowers from spring bulbs: above,
actea narcissus; left, yellow
tulips; right, gudoschnick tulips.

can be enjoyed during the blustery months of early spring should not be neglected. The diminutive flowers of snowdrops, glory-of-the-sun, scilla siberica, the very fragile winter aconite, and many others, while often tiny in size, have an extraordinary impact. Greenhouses and growers who produce the well-known, foil-wrapped pots of pink and blue hyacinths and red tulips could just as easily offer a hundred other, more wonderful kinds of bulbs and pot them in old mushroom boxes and strawberry crates, instead of in the deadly-looking plastic pots typically used. Daffodils, jonquils, and miniature narcissuses of all sorts are alternatives, as are the tiny blue (and rarer white) muscari hyacinths, specie tulips (often only four or five inches tall), and wood hyacinths. All of these are simple to grow right at home.

Late in the growing season, weeds and wildflowers grow in profusion, free for the taking. Along roadsides, along river banks, and dappling the fields grow Queen Anne's lace, butterfly weed, tickseed and other varieties of coreopsis, blue and white phlox, thistles, columbines, Indian paintbrush, black-eyed Susans, vivid purple lythrum, and hundreds of others. Nature's bounty, probably our greatest resource of all, is just waiting to be recognized, used, and enjoyed.

LEFT:
Gudoschnick and turkestanica tulips, red hyacinth, and stems of leucojum: a vivid yet delicate bouquet of flowers from spring bulbs.

RIGHT:
Perhaps the most delightful of the spring bulb flowers is the checkerboard lily, also known as miniature frittelaria or guinea hen flower.

CHAPTER FIVE : CONDITIONING

Water is a flower's life-support system.

A cut flower's capacity to drink water freely is the chief determinant of how long it will thrive.

Plants have vascular systems composed of conducting cells called xylem and phloem. This system is simpler than, but analogous to, the human cardiovascular system of veins, arteries, and capillaries. A flowering plant's vascular cells not only help to support the stem but also operate like a bundle of fine drinking straws, drawing water up to the leaves and to the flower itself. These cells must be kept open in order for water to flow freely.

While many of the techniques for conditioning flowers involve keeping the flowers well supplied with water, other environmental factors, notably humidity and temperature, pose hazards as well. A flower is composed mostly of water, and its vascular network is protected from the atmosphere only by very thin surfaces on stem, leaves, and petals. Therefore an excessively dry climate will imperil its life. Acting like a dry sponge, the air robs the flower of its moisture. Especially for the more delicate flowers, the more humid the environment, the longer the flower will live.

Aside from those tropical flowers that thrive on heat—bougainvillaea, for example, which actually requires heat to bloom properly—most flowers will last longer in cool, stable temperatures. This, of course, is why flower shops keep many of their cut flowers in temperature-controlled coolers. Excessive cold, however, can freeze a flower. Since the flower's vascular cells are filled with water (and as water freezes to ice, it expands), the cells burst, destroying the flower in the process.

Just as cool temperatures tend to stabilize most flowers, warmth will hasten their development. Light has a wonderful effect on many flowers; some, such as tulips, actually turn toward the light, even when cut and in a vase. Others, such as day lilies, morning glories, and crocuses open only in direct sunlight and close once the light has faded.

Light also affects the intensity of color in many types of flowers. Quince, forced

White and yellow gladiolas are brought down a few steps by editing. Their overpowering, specific, and inflexible qualities can be modified into softer features which more readily lend themselves to a mixed arrangement.

and flowering indoors away from direct sunlight, will produce delicate, pale pink petals. Branches from the same bush, left on the bush or developed in full sunlight, display the darker, almost coral-colored flowers we are familiar with.

Flowers that do not perform well once brought home from a flower shop, produce stand, or other commercial source have probably not been properly handled, either in shipping or at the retailer's. Most frequently, they have not been conditioned suitably and have been denied water somewhere along the line. Proper conditioning takes time and effort and therefore contributes to the eventual cost of the flower. Inexpensive flowers are rarely the bargain they are supposed to be, as they usually have been improperly cared for or bought late in the selling cycle—sometimes five or six days after they were cut.

A review of the basics for proper conditioning of flowers might be useful:

1. Avoid using scissors to cut flower stems; the scissors pinch the stem, inhibiting water intake.

2. Cut stems at an angle with a sharp knife; angling the cut exposes a greater area of the stem for water intake.

3. Immerse stems in water as soon as the cut is made; a newly cut stem begins to scale over immediately, reducing stem openings.

4. Allow stems to draw water for a few hours prior to arranging flowers.

5. Remove damaged and excessive foliage. For the most part, leaves should be removed below the water line. Leaves left on the stem can be conditioned under water for a few hours before use.

6. When cutting from the garden or elsewhere, take a container of water and put cut flowers in immediately; recondition later.

7. Cut either very early or very late in the day.

8. Mash or split the bottom two to three inches of tough, fibrous, or woody stems; scrape off the same amount of bark as well.

9. Avoid fouled water; change as often as seems necessary.

ABOVE:
The stem ends of Euphorbia
fulgens are seared in a candle
flame. Flowers that exude a thick
white sap—including all kinds of
euphorbias, poppies, poinsettias,
hollyhocks, plumeria, and Canter-
bury bells—need this treatment to
seal off the stem.

PAGES 98–99:
To facilitate their ability to drink in
water, thick and woody stems are
mashed with a mallet, opening up
the stem's vascular system. Here,
branches of hybrid white lilac are
being conditioned.

Certain flowers demand very specific conditioning treatments. Stems and branches that exude a sticky white sap when cut—two of the most common are poppies and euphorbia—need to have the fresh cut cauterized in order to prevent the loss of these vital fluids. This can be done either with fire, which sears the stem ends, or by scalding the stem ends in boiling water for a few seconds. In both cases, care should be taken not to injure the flowers themselves by exposure to excessive heat.

Flowers such as mimosa, which require a very humid environment to maintain their freshness, must be placed into a closed environment and allowed to develop; the plastic bag or other container should be removed just prior to the flower's use. A few hours in a normal environment quickly takes its toll, and although the somewhat shriveled flower clusters are still beautiful, their peak of freshness is lost.

Lilies present a unique problem: their long, luxurious anthers carry vividly colored heads of pollen. Although these certainly make the lily flower look more beautiful,

pollen that drops from the flowers can stain tablecloths, rugs, and clothing. Therefore it may be wise, in some cases, to remove the pollen before putting the lilies into a vase or an arrangement. The flower may even live somewhat longer if this delicate operation is performed.

Some flowers benefit greatly from being fully immersed in cool water for a few hours, allowing the entire stem, its leaves, and flowers the opportunity to drink in moisture. Camellia branches, rhododendrons, peonies, and some kinds of orchids all respond well to this procedure, especially if they have been cut and left out of water for more than a few hours. Roses that have wilted or whose heads have drooped can be soaked overnight in a tub of cool water, with a weight holding them well below the water line; their limp stems will regain their normal turgid state by the morning. Bunches of violets can also be "crisped up" by immersion in cool water for a few minutes.

❦

What you see is what you get, or so the old saying goes. But with a great many things in life, flowers included, this need not always be the case. Another conditioning treatment involves modifying flowers to suit the needs of an arrangement.

Sometimes it is just a question of altering a preconceived notion. For example, tradition dictates that flowers grown from bulbs—such as amaryllis, narcissus, hyacinth, and crocus—be planted in a pot with soil or, as in the case of paper-whites, grown in a low bowl with white stones. But the bulb is a major part of the plant, intriguing and beautiful in its own right; ridding it of its pot and washing it enables one to use the bulb in an entirely new way.

Most pot-grown bulbs develop in a very short time and are grown in a lightweight and loose medium. The roots grow extremely quickly and, unlike roots that have grown in the same pot for several years, they are easy to dislodge. Since all of the nourishment needed for the flower to develop is contained within the bulb itself, the absence of soil will not affect the flower at all. In fact, for the first season, the roots' principal function is simply to drink in water; their other role is simply

A bulb's flower—such as this amaryllis—can be transformed simply by washing away the dirt and exposing the bulb and root system.

to anchor the plant. If adequate water and an alternate means of support—such as a plant stake or a small branch—are provided, a bulb can exist without soil for the duration of the blooming period.

🙢

Techniques for washing bulbs vary. Twirling the bulb in a bucket of water is one way to do the trick. Another is to use the faucet at the sink. If the weather is mild enough, a hose outdoors also works well, and, although this may not sound attractive, one tried-and-true method is to hold the flower stem and place the bottom of the bulb in the toilet, flush, and let the swirling water do the job. As the roots are often brittle, care should be taken not to damage them.

A washed bulb, with its array of twisted roots and peeling sheaf of papery skin, can be placed in a simple glass cylinder or other suitable container, perhaps with a handful of beach pebbles or washed gravel loosely placed in and among the roots. It might also be impaled on a metal frog that has been stuck to the surface of a wide plate or shallow bowl. As long as water is provided to the root system, the flower will continue to thrive.

🙢

One can actually alter the physical shape of a flower with a process we might term "editing." Large flowers can thereby be reduced in size and mass and rendered less assertive, better able to harmonize with other flowers.

Any flower with multiple blooms can be edited. Gladiolas, for example, can be changed dramatically by snapping off the top two-thirds of the stalk. The gladiola, once tall and spiky, is now shapely and compact and has a softness and workability its more extenuated form lacked. With the overwhelming presence of the stem reduced, the individual flowers become the focus of attention, and their pleasing shape and subtle coloration can be more fully appreciated.

Other spiky flowers—such as delphinium, larkspur, stock, and tall snapdragons—can also be trimmed, not only from the top but from the center as well, thereby decreasing the flower's density or bulk. Changed from a tall shaft of continuous

An amaryllis plays a different role once its bulb and root system have been washed (left). For one thing, the visible bulb offers a mass to balance that of the enormous flower. Furthermore, although its massive blossoms often dominate other flowers, a little inventive editing can reduce the scale of an amaryllis to something more manageable (right).

PAGE 106:
As with the euphorbias, poppies need to be cauterized at the base. This can be accomplished by scorching the stem ends in a bunch.

PAGE 107:
Individual gladiolus blossoms strung together on a lei—a fanciful outcome of the editing process.

flowers to a smattering of individual flowers along its stem, delphinium acquires an entirely different presence—the individual blooms can really be seen. Another drastic way to make such a full, massive flower dainty and airy is to strip off all but a small crown of flowers at the top.

Many chrysanthemums are multiflowered and can be scaled down by removing a few of the flower heads. Similarly, stems of lilies often grow so dense with flowers that they cannot be considered for a mixed arrangement in their natural state. But removing a few flowers makes the stem much more workable. Even a feathery spray of tiny orchids may be a more insistent presence than one needs and can be lightened by editing. Most multiflowered orchids, vandas for instance, produce branched flower stems. Since many of the flowers face in different directions, those facing inward can be removed in favor of those facing out, thereby sharpening the impact of the whole and improving its visual legibility.

All of the flowering branches—quince, cherry, magnolia, forsythia, euphorbia, and so on—may profit by selective pruning, either to reduce their total impact or to remove a part of the branch that heads off in the wrong direction or that does not contribute to a beautiful linear shape. For instance, a branch of seeded eucalyptus is often too visually prominent to work well in an arrangement, but it can become a much more subtle and harmonious presence if most of the leaves are taken off, thus exposing the seed clusters to view.

Finally, when more curvilinear flowers seem to be called for, flowers that appear to be too straight to be of use can sometimes be "coaxed" into a more lyrical disposition by carefully bending the stem again and again. Conversely, flowers too droopy to be used can often be straightened by being carefully wrapped in wet newspaper and soaked in cold water to help the stems regain their turgidity.

Wilted roses spend a night soaking in cool water, weighted down so that they stay fully immersed. By morning, the stems are turgid again, the flowers alert and revived.

CHAPTER SIX : CONTAINERS

Anything that holds water can be a container for flowers.

Even an object that doesn't hold water on its own can easily be lined with something that does. Although many people actually go to the trouble of having galvanized liners made to order by a tin-knocker or metalsmith to fit a favorite basket or slightly derelict urn, tumblers, Dixie Cups, Tupperware bowls, and other everyday vessels accomplish the same end—with a little less finesse, perhaps, but with completely satisfactory results nonetheless.

Often the design or style of a container will suggest the kinds of flowers most appropriate for it. For example, a rustic well bucket or a green-blue canning jar seems to call for a rather casual assortment of weeds, wildflowers, or garden flowers. A small butter crock or a wooden grain measure suggests a handful of herbs or a bunch or two of pansies or sweet peas. A vintage Art Deco vase, on the other hand, demands artfully arranged, elegant, and stylish flowers—calla lilies, desert candles, shapely stems of ranunculus, fringed carnations, or hot-poker flowers, also known as tritoma.

The size and shape of a container, together with the nature of its opening, determine the ease with which it will accommodate flowers. Generally speaking, the narrower the mouth of the vase, the easier it will be to arrange a selection of flowers and hold it in place. Of course, an opening of an inch or two will take only a few flowers, but a slightly larger mouth works well for a mixed arrangement of modest proportions. Wide-mouthed vases, on the other hand, can hold great quantities of flowers but lack the means to keep them in position. Except for flowers that have some real mass lower on their stems—tulips whose lower leaves are intact, for example—most flowers simply collapse to the sides of such a vase, defying proper placement.

Certain distinctive containers—for instance, a modern vase styled in sharp angles and flattened sides, or designed in concentric circles or in other geometric shapes—seem to require an assortment of flowers assertive enough to stand up to the container. More neutrally shaped vases, such as the classic ginger jar, the

This chameleon vase, a souvenir picked up in the streets of Guadalajara, looks whimsically festive with tulips, pink calla lilies, yellow sandersonii, and ranunculus.

Transparent, tinted hand-blown glass vases hold apricot tulips—delicacy of curve and color in a perfect marriage.

ABOVE:
Orchids are epiphytes; they don't need soil, just moisture from the air, to thrive. These wall boxes approximate their natural tropical forest habitat, where orchids anchor themselves to the lofty branches of trees.

simple cylinder, and the globe, can accommodate a far wider range of possibilities.

The ideal shape for a mixed arrangement seems to be that of the ginger jar. This age-old form has an appropriately sized opening and an ample interior, which allows stems to be placed at the necessary angles to one another to construct and maintain a well-rounded arrangement. In contrast, a cylindrical container tends to restrict stems to an upright position. A spherical container presents difficulties that are more visual than physical; a round arrangement often appears to mimic the globelike container below, whereas an irregularly shaped or oblong arrange- ment sometimes appears a little top-heavy or lopsided. But the vertical aspect of the ginger-jar form, whether classically proportioned or elongated, diminishes this problem, making a satisfactory arrangement far easier to achieve.

Shallow containers pose another kind of problem, for they provide little or no support for the stems and usually require a device such as a metal frog to secure the flowers in place. Since these holders are usually small and their capacity limited, the ways in which flowers can be positioned relative to one another are restricted. And while this treatment is appropriate to a few kinds of flowers and to a more stylized approach to arranging, the result often appears forced or contrived.

Curiously enough, many vases that are supposedly designed specifically to hold flowers do not do so easily. Fine crystal vases of all shapes and descriptions rarely have an appropriate opening or a properly shaped interior and therefore do not readily welcome an arrangement of flowers. One of the best-known vases, the celebrated Aalto vase, with its extremely wide, fjordlike shape, requires masses of flowers, since too few flowers simply fall gracelessly around the edges. A handful of flowers—among them, poppies, anemones, freesia, ranunculus, and tulips—can look extremely handsome in this vase when used by themselves and in sufficient quantities. However, flowers of a less lyrical nature simply crowd the vase and obscure its distinctive form.

Other considerations when selecting a container include color, texture, and patina, mostly matters of personal preference. The colors of flowers and their containers

An early American hand-painted wooden box is an eccentric—yet somehow completely appropriate— container for the bright dwarf zinnias.

RIGHT:
An old-fashioned Mason jar
provides another ideal shape
for flowers.

BELOW:
Morella roses in an
armadillo-skin holder.

LEFT:
An armload of garish garden zinnias stuffed into a gleaming copper fish poacher.

ABOVE:
Full-blown garden roses in a classic Oriental ginger jar. Many flowers can be accommodated by this shape; its relatively narrow mouth and expansive midsection are ideally suited to both long and short stems. The vase's deep, subtle glaze offers additional pleasure.

RIGHT:
Art Deco designers loved flowers, and it is still relatively easy to find Deco vases in most flea markets and antique shops. Even when the color of the vase is subdued, only a strong flower will hold its own against the line. Here, stylized ranunculus provide a high-contrast, almost cartoonish air.

should harmonize, unless a deliberately jarring effect is desired. Therefore, the crimson roses appropriate to a cobalt blue or gunmetal gray container might not work so well in a vase of lemon yellow or lime green. The surface of an opaque vase is worth considering as well. The cheap, highly glossed vases that one sees so often seem somehow unworthy of the delicate shades of the flowers they are to hold, whereas glazes with depth, mystery, and subtlety can establish an immediate rapport with their occupants. And the patina of a vase that comes with age and wear lends personality and individuality. Tarnish does not always have to be rubbed off a silver vase, for example; at times it might be more appropriate for such a container to have a pewtery appearance. Similarly, copper develops a beautiful, blue-green discoloration; wood gains character as it absorbs the oils of the hands that touch it; and terra-cotta pots pick up a marvelous, uneven gray-green cast, a result of the salts that have leached out of the soil the pots have held over a period of time.

LEFT:
A spring-flowering clematis entwined on a shapely branch serves as a table centerpiece.

RIGHT:
Bulbs of late-blooming autumn crocus do just fine on a glass plate; their nourishment and moisture comes entirely from the bulbs.

ABOVE AND RIGHT:
On a window sill that serves as a
potting ledge, tiny myrtle trees are
transferred from plastic pots to
miniature rose pots of red clay.
Note the moss in the pots, which
helps to convey the comfortable
impression that plant and pot have
been together for a long time.

Mädderlake searches greenhouses, barns, and nurseries for a
variety of pots—looking especially
for different textures and shapes
and for the fine quality of age.

Tex

PAGES 124–125:
It is not always necessary, or even desirable, to clean and scour clay pots. A patina of moss, silt, and fungi does not indicate disease but is a natural, and to many eyes attractive, condition of age and weathering.

LEFT:
Almost obscuring this antique weather vane is a Lygodium japonicum, better known as a climbing fern—one of the very few vining ferns known. The pot, in turn, is nearly obscured by baby's tears. Like partridgeberry, various mosses, grasses, and some small weeds, baby's tears form a low ground cover that can make pots look "lived in."

RIGHT (TOP):
A simple herb—a rosemary prostratus—is wonderful in an old pot.

RIGHT (CENTER):
An unusually tall lady-slipper orchid has been playfully set into a tiny clay collander.

RIGHT (BOTTOM):
Clematis is a long, leggy vine flower. Here it has been potted in terra cotta, and twined around the pot so that the flowers cluster together and unite pot with plant. (Eventually, this beautiful vine should be planted in the garden, near an arbor or bush that it can climb.)

RIGHT:
In a contemporary water pitcher, a very old-fashioned heap of mimosa, white peony tulips, rambling roses, miniature narcissus, and pink and white garden roses.

BELOW:
A small, simple white vase is the perfect foil for velvety cattleya orchids.

A most unusual tiered vase looks striking with these wide-awake gerbera daisies (right). Another stylized vase takes well to the tropical opulence of gladiolas (left).

LEFT:
Perfect balance of line, color, and style: a small frosted glass vase with pink cyclamen flowers.

BELOW:
The sweet romanticism of this diminutive Cupid vase with crackle glaze lends itself perfectly to a fragrant bunch of lily-of-the-valley.

RIGHT:
Mädderlake's own version of the classic Oriental ginger jar, with strewn flowers reflected in its mirror-like glaze.

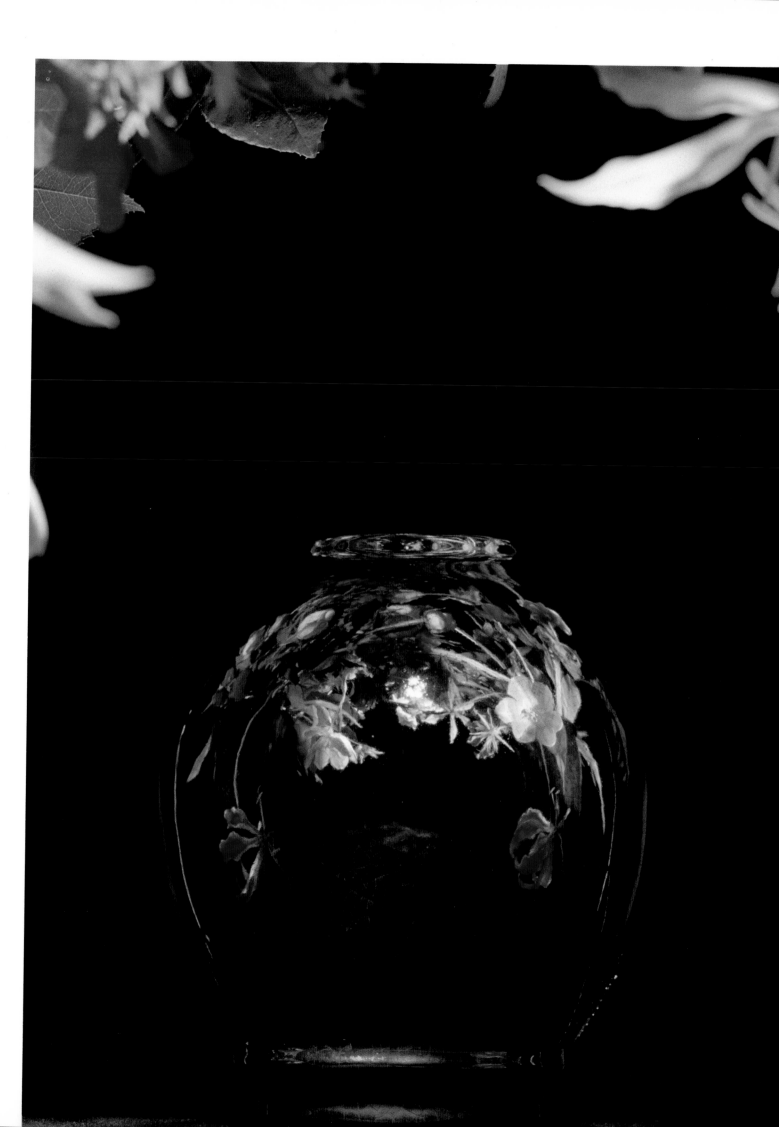

Making an amaryllis feel at home. From the florist's plastic pot, it is removed to an English orchid pot, placed a little off-center and topped with moss. Then, the supporting stake is replaced with a branch of cornelian cherry. The leaves are repositioned, and the tiny bulb at the plant's base is exposed. These small, easily executed changes make a dramatic difference.

CHAPTER SEVEN : ARRANGEMENTS

The ultimate aim of any arrangement of flowers is to achieve a perfect union—among the various flowers themselves, and between the flowers and the container that is to hold them.

No matter how simple or complex this union is to be, whether commonplace or bizarre, understated or melodramatic, it must wed the various elements into a coherent and inevitable-looking whole. Many factors govern this process; some are intuitive, but many others can be learned.

It takes at least four or five different kinds of flowers to create a true mixed arrangement. A couple of dozen of the same flower, or a handful of two or three different kinds, is more a casual grouping of flowers and generally looks best if arranged somewhat haphazardly. By contrast, combining a number of dissimilar flowers is a more complicated matter and requires somewhat more thought and attention.

Personal preference is the place to begin: if the flowers do not appeal, they will not provide inspiration. Availability should be checked, for what is fresh at a given moment may often suggest the direction to take. A little arithmetic is needed, too. The sizes and quantities of the flowers should be calculated, and consideration must be given not only to the shape and capacity of the container to be used, but also to the setting in which the flowers are to be placed and the reason the arrangement is being made. For example, a high-ceilinged foyer that needs to be highlighted for a party will probably require something grand and imposing, while the same foyer may call for a far simpler treatment on a more intimate occasion. Flowers should look appropriate both to the place and to the moment.

There are two different approaches to working with flowers. In the first, which can be described as casual, the natural inclinations of the flowers themselves suggest how they are to be used. In the other—a studied, more interpretative approach—a few flowers are singled out and placed into very carefully determined relationships to one another, sometimes representationally evoking such images as the earth, the land, and the sky and at other times simply describing abstract shapes. The Japanese art of flower arranging, *ikebana*, is probably the purest expression

This unusual Art Deco vase has many extra openings along the sides, allowing for a more adventuresome bouquet. The flowers already in place have sketched the outline that other flowers will fill in.

of this second approach, and its many derivations can be seen in the highly stylized arrangements of tropical flowers and exotic foliage so prevalent today.

More casual or natural arrangements of flowers can be divided into two broad categories. In one, the flowers are placed cheek by jowl, resulting in the overstuffed bouquets that the Victorians favored; in the other, the flowers are combined with a lighter touch, leaving plenty of space within the arrangement. The former often uses more lavish, blowsy flowers such as huge garden roses, tuberous begonias, parrot tulips, delphiniums, stock, hybrid lilies, and snapdragons, all seemingly jammed to capacity in the vase. The latter is often composed of flowers such as jonquils, sweet peas, many types of flowering branches, weeds and wildflowers, coreopsis, Queen Anne's lace, and other flowers of a smaller scale or a more delicate nature. Rather than a lavish, overblown effect, a gentle layering of flowers is sought here, inviting visual exploration of all the mysteries contained within.

Like a building, an arrangement of flowers has the architectural requirement of a firm foundation. Rather than using chicken wire, floral foam, or some other device that must be hidden from view, one can secure flowers within a container both simply and naturally. A strong and firm base needs to be constructed with a low center of gravity that will anchor the arrangement in the vase, to keep it from tipping over or coming apart. One of the simplest ways to make such a foundation is to wedge a small branch or several sturdy stems into a vase, forming a cradle into which the flowers can be placed. Once three or four flowers have been added and locked into this structure, the arrangement is secure.

Another kind of cradle can be made from a sturdy tulip and one other flower with a firm stem. Because the lower leaf of the tulip is both heavy and pliable, it can be draped over the side of the vase, firmly holding the tulip in place. The second flower is then inserted diagonally into the vase from an opposing direction, piercing the leaf and coming to rest against the side of the vase, forming an "X" that locks the two flowers together and forms a solid connection to the vase.

RIGHT:
One of the best ways to begin building a secure base for a flower arrangement is by wedging a branch into the container. Doing so will provide not only a low center of gravity but also places for flower stems to lodge. The best, like this piece of crab apple, have numerous crotches, which afford many possibilities.

PAGE 140:
When the flowers have been carefully introduced into the arrangement by the rotation method (that is, turning the container constantly as one works), their stems weave together in a secure web. And the arrangement will have a loose and natural, asymmetrical but balanced, look as a result.

PAGE 141:
Ideally, a well-built arrangement should be able to withstand being turned upside down without falling apart. Once turned upright, this assortment will return to approximately its original shape.

This classic mixed arrangement (left) uses an elaborately large number of flowers—seventeen in all—without becoming preposterous and without any one flower up-staging the others. It includes a large branch laden with Valencia oranges; a long branch cut from a Cissus rotundifolia; anemone, stock, calendula, and vallota; amaryllis, rose, ranunculus, rieger begonia, and pumpkin lily; two kinds of orchids—oncidium and cattleya; polypodium fern, yellow jasmine, crab apple, and purple akebia berries; and some almost-spent flowers from a false sea onion plant. The overall effect of this eclectic mix is one of whimsical grandeur.

After a week or so, most of the flowers have had it. But a new arrangement (right) can be built from the old. Change the water, discard all the spent flowers, judiciously prune and salvage the orange, the akebia, the false sea onion, and the cissus—and one can begin again. Into the new arrange-ment will go yellow kangaroo paws and branches of red and black berries.

PAGES 144–145:
Peering within this arrangement, we see witch hazel, cornflowers, miniature cymbidium, muscari, purple hyacinth, viburnum, and anemone. The outer layer shows gloriosa lily, quince, barberry, and yellow euphorbia. Unlike the standard, all-on-the-surface arrange-ments, this kind of layered, dense yet airy group of flowers offers endless surprise, complexity, and beauty within.

PAGES 146–147:
The stems of flowers, often hidden from view, can have a mysterious beauty all their own and may be an integral visual part of the arrangement.

Filling a basket on the window sill are thistles from the fields and vallota, pink belladonna, and white lilies from the garden. Through the screen's haze come the hum of insects, the heavy smell of flowers—a sweet, sleepy summer afternoon in the country.

With their thorns intact and a few intermediate leaves left on, three or four roses cut at different heights and placed in the vase from opposing directions also form a secure base, provided that at least one of them is cut short enough to establish a low center of gravity.

Once this foundation has been created, the basic shape or outline of the arrangement can be established by placing the two or three most important flowers into an interesting relationship to each other and to the flowers that form the base. As subsequent flowers are added, the vase should be rotated, so that the arrangement is not created from only one vantage point. Even an arrangement that is specifically intended to be placed on a shelf or table, in front of a wall, or to be seen from just one side should be constructed with a sense of the three-dimensional effect in mind.

❦

The foliage in an arrangement should come from the flowers themselves. Green bases of fern fronds and lemon and huckleberry leaves, from which leafless stems of flowers seem to spring, usually hide a large brick of floral foam or a crumpled wad of chicken wire. Making a natural base eliminates the need for this excess greenery, for there is no longer anything to be hidden. Should a brick of foam be required—as with certain low arrangements made for a table centerpiece, for instance—bits and pieces of foliage from the flowers should disguise it, not unrelated greenery. For example, if roses are to be used, the lower leaves, which would otherwise be discarded, can be used to cover the brick. And for all flower arrangements, care should be taken when deciding which leaves are to be left on and which are to be removed; the interior of an arrangement is easily obscured by too much foliage, and it is difficult to cut off lower leaves once the arrangement is almost complete.

An arrangement of flowers should have visual movement and rhythm. It should not be so simple that it can be taken in all at once. Rather, it should be complex enough to stimulate visual discovery. A symmetrical array of flowers is expected, predictable, and therefore often boring. It is far more interesting to place flowers

into dynamic rather than static balance. With an asymmetrical approach, one move is countered by another that is of equivalent value but not exactly the same. Two or three small flowers can balance a single larger one; a craggy branch on one side of the vase may have its counterpart in a parrot tulip on the other; a cluster of berries can balance a brightly colored anemone. The addition of each flower affects all of the others, and the arrangement is brought into and thrown out of balance until it is finally perfect.

LEFT:
A full summery arrangement: tall delphiniums, roses of all kinds, anemones, gloriosa lilies, and freesia—combined with a branch or two of flowering clematis and a snipping from a purple streptocarpus plant.

RIGHT:
Delphiniums dominate this arrangement of black-eyed Susan, sunflowers, Queen Anne's lace, dahlias, honeysuckle, rose hips, and weigela.

BELOW:
All white—but so many different shades, textures, and shapes: iris, gardenia, cyclamen, anemone, geranium, narcissus, stock, lilac, ranunculus, peperomia, and ornithigalum flowers.

BOTTOM:
A very personal wedding bouquet. Among the barnyard animals are the white allium, white nicotiana, roses, and orange-cupped narcissuses that Gilda Radner carried down the aisle.

RIGHT:
On the table with a summer lunch are many colors of sweet pea, Queen Anne's lace, rambling rose, brodeia, ranunculus, and campanula flowers.

PAGES 154–155:
Breakfast stays sunny with these ixia, white allium, ranunculus, sweet pea, delphinium, bachelor's-button, rose, and tuberose blossoms crammed into a Navaho pot.

LEFT:
Relaxed luxury from another time—in the Flemish style.

LEFT:
A "dead-of-the-winter" wildflower mix built as a low centerpiece for a table. Cornflowers, privet berries, miniature scabious, Euphorbia fulgens (trimmed down), rosemary prostratus in flower, nerine, crispas, poppies, cyclamen leaves, and peperomia cut from a house plant.

ABOVE:
A single-color arrangement can be very dramatic. Here, rieger begonias, gloriosa lilies, tulips, euphorbias, and red orchids and berries flame out of their vase.

RIGHT:
Hybrid white lilac, cut short, has been combined in a tight, fragrant, seductive mix with pernettya berries, purple eugenia, and blue hyacinth.

BELOW:
This odd, playful floral grouping mixes two kinds of hyacinth—standard and the tiny muscari variety—with a flashy orchid stem.

LEFT:
Large, strong flowers need to balance with others like them to keep harmony in a mix. These birthday flowers—a sunflower, delphiniums, auratum lilies, pink belladonnas, a stem of montbretia, a tuberose, and orange vallota— convey an air of celebration.

ABOVE:
In a fanciful setting by a lake, this grouping of flowers has all the languor and wildness of the countryside. The stretching stems of white alba lilies, the white hydrangea, lady's-slippers, liz-zianthus, belladonna lilies, cosmos, roses, wild sweet pea flowers, a single tuberose, and an orange neomarica, largely gone to seed, meet in a mad tumble.

PAGES 164–165:
Mace's dilemma: peach tulips, gloriosa lilies, yellow callas, calendula poppies, hybrid Queen Anne's lace, and white dendrobium orchids.

CHAPTER EIGHT: SETTINGS

Fresh flowers bring life into a room.

Unlike the other elements that surround us—tables and chairs, curtains and rugs, objects that can be changed only with great difficulty and at great expense—cut flowers come and go easily, sporting new colors, evoking new moods, marking special occasions. They can bring the garden or woods into the house, filling the indoors with the sights and smells of nature, reminding us of the season at hand or the one longed for. Thus a simple jar of bright yellow jonquils perched on a kitchen window sill in the winter sits blissfully unaware of the frost on the glass or the bitter cold outside. An armload of freshly cut lilacs fills the entire house with its heady scent. The sweet and sylvan smell of a handful of lilies-of-the-valley, placed on a bedside table, is a reminder of the morning's walk.

Flowers are not just for company. They are the stuff of everyday life as well as of special moments; they offer us too much to be relegated only to social occasions. Flowers also belong to the times when we're alone. They have an equal place on the dining table, the kitchen table, and the kitchen counter. Just as a glass of sherry is for the enjoyment of the cook as well as the embellishment of the sauce, so flowers can enliven the hours we spend preparing for guests as well as the time we spend entertaining them.

Whether lavish or simple and understated, flowers should be appropriate to the setting in which they are to be placed. The more specific the environment, the more restricted the possibilities for suitable flowers. A wide-open loft space with few details and a spare architectural character can accommodate flowers ranging from romantic to bizarre; they can be appropriately put into almost any conceivable vase or container of any size, however extreme. By contrast, an impeccably furnished Georgian drawing room practically *requires* certain kinds of vases, certain types of flowers, and a specific manner of arranging them. Pale white roses in a low silver bowl or a small garden bouquet in a Minton pitcher would work perfectly in such surroundings, while an Early American stoneware crock of field flowers, a rustic

Creamy, pale-pink nerines in simple glass vases enhance this elegant, serene setting.

LEFT:
This bouquet was arranged loosely to resemble a wildflower bouquet. As Lady Bird Johnson said, "An arrangement of flowers should be airy enough for a bird to fly right through it."

BELOW:
The huge nineteenth-century painting and grand piano are indeed on a grand scale. And the branchy flowers, though also imposing, have been arranged in an open fashion, so as not to obscure the painting.

basket of French tulips, or a stainless steel vase with stalks of ginger or anthurium flowers would look out of place. Most decisions about suitability of flowers and containers to their surroundings can be governed by common sense.

Flowers are just one of the many elements that make up an interior, and thus, in general, they should play a supporting role rather than a leading one. For truly festive occasions, flowers can be given center stage, enhancing the special air of celebration that characterizes the event. But more often than not, flowers should quietly heighten the atmosphere or character of a room without calling undue attention to themselves.

Flowers may contribute to the feeling of a whole room—as, for instance, when large, sensuous white calla lilies are placed squarely on the grand piano, or when a large bowl of pink and white peonies is set in the middle of the coffee table. Or they may subtly grace a small part of the room, such as a mantel, a tabletop, or a window sill—not apparent at first glance, but discovered in good time. Diminutive flowers need an appropriate setting and work very well when grouped with a few small objects into a little vignette. A tiny blue vase of grape hyacinths, which would have no impact in a large room, finds a fitting home on a small table with a delicate silver picture frame, a favorite old book, and a miniature wooden box.

❦

When selecting flowers, as when choosing clothing or make-up, or composing a menu, it is important to remember that displays that are too self-conscious or conspicuous betray poor taste. Just as the oversauced, overflamed, overwrought dishes so prevalent a few years back have given way to simple and honest fare made from the freshest and most interesting and varied ingredients, so ideas about flowers can follow suit. Common sense endorses the oft-quoted axiom "less is more." Simplicity carries its own elegance; subtlety often provides far more delight than does showiness.

Dinner parties especially seem to call for flowers, and generally right in the center of the table. Even people who rarely buy or use flowers tend to feel the need

RIGHT:
For a high-style room with inlaid
furniture and shiny fabrics, one
might expect a full, overblown
arrangement of flowers. But here,
the unexpected: a casual, woodsy
gathering.

BELOW:
These delphiniums have been
thinned out along the stem so that
they will not block the painting,
whose blue color and fluffy out-
lines they echo.

LEFT:
Since orchid flowers are best seen at eye level—the flowers droop so—one excellent place to put them is on a mantel.

BELOW:
So far, only the anchoring hawthorn branches have been placed in this polished stone urn. The rest of the flowers are yet to come.

PAGE 178
A wreath of bittersweet berries adorns a wrought iron gate in New York City.

PAGE 179:
One of life's great pleasures is finding new places to set flowers. Here a brilliant, airy bouquet fills a recessed window on a courtyard.

Although most of the carnations at fruit stands and in shops are drab, if not dyed, these cream-colored and vivid orange carnations are extraordinary and full of character.

for flowers on the table when they entertain. But a dinner party is, first and foremost, a gathering devoted to food, drink, and good company. Everything that pertains to the occasion, of which flowers are but one element, should support the whole event and work together to create one harmonious mood or feeling.

Generally a dinner is conceived around an idea about the food and how it is to be served, and although flowers usually go hand in hand with this idea, at times they are simply not appropriate to the table. A lobster feast, for example, served directly on a table covered with layers of newspaper, finds its centerpiece first in the steaming platter of lobsters heaped on top of one another, later in the pile of shells that remains. Although tankards of ale and dishes of melted butter are an integral part of the event, flowers are not. Similarly, other food conceived as the focal point of the meal, such as a huge bouillabaisse or a steaming cassoulet, may rule out flowers on the table. At these times, the flowers that grace the eve ning can be placed on a nearby mantel, sideboard, or window sill, lending their presence to the room but not the table. Wherever they are placed, and however prominently, flowers should look personal and spontaneous, not commercial and contrived.

❧

Surrounded as we often are by a world of glass, metal, asphalt, and plastic, we need flowers in our midst to reconnect us to the quiet, pure beauty of the natural world. Swept up in an ever-faster-paced electronic society, we need the presence of flowers to bring us back down to earth, to give us momentary pause and respite from the frenetic tempo of modern life. Considering all the ways in which flowers can enrich our surroundings, uplift our spirits, and even speak for us in our absence, the time has come for us to shed our old, outdated notions of what flowers are all about and to rediscover the virtually limitless possibilities they offer.

LA TENTATION DE SAINT ANTOINE   74
Détail du volet droit (pl. 9)
LA TABLE MAGIQUE

TOP:
Branches of flowers cut from rieger begonia plants.

ABOVE:
A private still-life: flowers arranged in an etched glass caviar dish.

LEFT:
Flowers can belong to a whole room, or to just part of it—as in this small-scale environment of a secretary desk with a vanda orchid.

RIGHT:
Flowers glimpsed from the street.

BELOW:
A classic candelabra on the dining table frames a romantic mix of flowers.

BELOW AND RIGHT:
The rich textures of French lilac
and viburnum enliven an otherwise
austere environment.

PAGES 188–189:
The voluptuous curves and sug-
gestive scent of hybrid white and
pale purple lilacs mimic the hectic
patterns in a painting by Robert
Gwathmey.

PAGES 190–191:
Soft, dense clusters of rambling
roses pressed into an undulating
glass vase.

LEFT AND BELOW:
These anthuriums have an unusually floppy, flexible quality that gives them a playful, lively aspect. They fit uncannily well into a fifties setting.

ABOVE:
An old mortar holds numerous stems of white phaleonopsis orchids for a studied, powerful effect in a corporate board room.

RIGHT:
A washed narcissus bulb and flower in a clean tall glass cylinder— a fresh, stark presence in the bathroom.

PAGE 196:
Simple glass containers hold their own in a tablesetting of period glassware and china.

PAGE 197:
One of the ways that flowers can work with their environment is by creating a balanced discord. Into this serene, pastel room a very striking arrangement has been placed: vegetables, fruits, and flowers impaled on branches.

PAGES 198–199:
An alternative to a centerpiece might be these brilliantly colored vanda orchids placed around the table. Their exotic color and shape provide an exciting, if slightly jarring, contrast to staid, classic candlesticks.

LEFT:
An extraordinary harpsichord forms the backdrop for the romance of a simple vase of white eustoma.

RIGHT:
An amaryllis sent as a gift becomes part of a table-top grouping.

LEFT:
A tableau: the new apartment, Chinese take-out, and jonquils from a local produce stand in a yogurt container. Flowers begin to make a house a home.

BELOW:
Full-blown tulips preside over the work table.

For the cook's eyes only: trumpet lilies from the garden (left), and a simple crock of skimmia flowers (below).

Christmas in the country: a field-grown balsam, with its open, irregular branches, offers a lot of room for ornaments, including floral decorations made of different kinds of nerines.

RIGHT:
Pumpkin-colored trumpet lilies and three other hybrid lilies in a crystal vase at a dining-table-turned-work-table.

ABOVE:
Late afternoon light through a lace curtain dapples the white cosmos.

LEFT:
Sunlight streams through colored decanters filled with garden roses.

BELOW:
Branches cut from a flowering pomegranate, with their restrained but forceful curves and muted coloration, balance beautifully with an architectural drawing by Piranesi.

ABOVE AND RIGHT:
Another variation on the centerpiece: while snow falls outdoors,
a cozy meal is brightened by
primroses potted in old copper
saucepans.

PAGE 214:
Even at the quietest, most intimate
moments, flowers can animate a
room. Roses by the bed are one
delightful example.

PAGE 215:
A vignette of miniatures: muscari,
dwarf cyclamen, lily-of-the-valley,
and cuphea flowers. (The wooden
matchsticks indicate scale.)

The strange brown hues of these vanda orchids are underscored by placing them in old-fashioned brown glass apothecary jars (left).

LEFT:
A profusion of flowers—including pink callas; white, pink, and red nerines; dwarf clianthus; poppies; anemones; and hyacinths—is readied for use around the house.

BELOW:
Flowers by the bucket, from the city's flower markets.

BOTTOM:
A redware jug holds hollyhocks, roses, cyclamen flowers, and barberry branches.

LEFT:
An arrangement that has been left out in the cool air of an autumn morning is retrieved in time for lunch.

PAGE 222:
The stems of hyacinths, like those of tulips and other bulb flowers, actually elongate in water. These drooping, fragrant hyacinths are a casual presence at lunch.

PAGE 223:
Flaming parrot tulips—ravishing colors in an old enamelled pitcher.

PAGE 224:
The shadow of a scabious flower falls across an attic bedroom.

PAGE 225:
An old clock and pictures under the stairs. The tiny pitcher with flowers is only incidental to the fullness of life.

Roses can be as formal—or as casual—as the occasion.

A simple arrangement of delphinium flowers, pansies, and hyacinths makes a serene still life.

PHOTO CREDITS

Langdon Clay: 1, 8, 21 24, 25, 26–27, 31, 33, 34–35, 40, 46–47, 55, 58–59, 62, 74–75, 78–79, 88–89, 94, 97, 98–99, 100, 103, 106, 107, 110, 120, 124–125, 132, 133, 134, 135, 139, 140, 141, 143, 144–145, 164–165, 166, 170, 171, 172, 180, 188–189, 194, 195, 196, 197, 198–199, 200, inside back flap

Michael Geiger: 2, 5, 10, 20, 36B, 39, 44, 56–57, 66, 67, 70, 71, 73, 76, 77, 80, 81, 82, 83, 90, 91, 92, 93, 108, 112, 115, 118, 119T, 121, 122T, 123, 126, 127, 128, 149, 150, 151, 162, 163, 178, 179, 185, 208, 220, 224

John Dugdale: 12, 16–17, 18, 19, 36T, 37, 43, 45, 60, 72, 84, 85, 86, 104, 113, 116, 117, 119B, 122B, 129, 160, 161, 182, 183B, 186, 187, 203, 204, 206, 207, 212, 213, 214, 216, 217, 218, 219, 222, 223, 225, 226, 228, front cover, back cover

Brian Hagiwara: 28, 29, 38, 48, 49, 54, 63, 64, 105, 142, 146–147, 152T, 153, 156, 158, 159, 168, 169, 174, 175, 176, 177, 183T, 184, 201, 202, 205, 209, 210, 211, 215

Adam Bartos: 154–155

ACKNOWLEDGMENTS

Mrs. Paul Mellon, for her continuing inspiration

Mr. and Mrs. Ralph Davidson
The Reverend Davis Given
Bette Ann and Charles Gwathmey
Bruce Kovner and Sarah Peter
Alan Lindenfeld
Michael Larocca
Jo Carole Lauder
Paul Newman and Joanne Woodward
Dara and Mark Perlbinder
Phillip Pfeiffer
Lock Whitney
Eric Bernard

International Paper Company
The National Gallery of Art
The Pierpont Morgan Library

Heidi Gurbarg
Terrance and Martin Koeniges
Al and Cathy Possehl
Gilda Weinstein
Karen Zendig

Maxine Bargrasser
David Caskie
Ibi Hinrichs
David Parish
Steve Rascoe
Jim Wilson
Robert Wilson

and especially,
John Kelly

Design by Mary Shanahan

The text was set in Gill sans by Arkotype Inc., New York, New York. The
book was printed and bound by Toppan Printing Company, Ltd., Tokyo, Japan.